For Kaileia, dedicated to her hockey journey

SLAPSHOT SISTERS BOOK 1: Emma's New Hometown

Title: Slapshot Sisters Book 1: Emma's New Hometown
Author: Daniel Pasternack
Publisher: Kindle Direct Publishing
Website: www.slapshotsisters.com

First Edition

All rights reserved. No part of this publication may be reproduced, distributed, or transmitted in any form or by any means, including photocopying, recording, or other electronic or mechanical methods, without the prior written permission of the publisher, except in the case of brief quotations embodied in critical reviews and certain other noncommercial uses permitted by copyright law.

ISBN: 9798868458545

Names: Pasternack, Daniel, author.
Title: Slapshot Sisters Book 1: Emma's New Hometown / by Daniel Pasternack.
Description: First Edition. | Las Vegas: Kindle Direct Publishing, 2023 | Series: Slapshot Sisters; Book 1
Subjects: BISAC: Juvenile Fiction / Sports & Recreation / Hockey. Juvenile Fiction / Social Themes / New Experience.

The characters and events in this book are fictitious. Any similarity to real persons, living or dead, is coincidental and not intended by the author.

Cover design by SusansArt

12/2023
First Edition

For information about special discounts for bulk purchases, please contact Daniel Pasternack at the website above.

For more information about the author and upcoming books in the series, visit www.slapshotsisters.com or www.danielspasternack.com.

Table of Contents

CHAPTER 1: NEW IN TOWN 4

CHAPTER 2: THE FIRST PRACTICE 15

CHAPTER 3: GETTING INTO A ROUTINE 29

CHAPTER 4: ZOE 41

CHAPTER 5: CHARLOTTE 52

CHAPTER 6: ARIEL 65

CHAPTER 7: GAMEDAY 76

CHAPTER 8: THE FIRST SCRIMMAGE 88

APPENDIX: LIST OF CHARACTERS 107

Chapter 1: New in Town

Emma Kimura had just moved from the cold city of Toronto to Las Vegas, a city where the sun blazed with an intensity she wasn't accustomed to. It was August and she had never felt anything like the heat that was cooking her on a daily basis.

Whenever she stepped outside, the hot air felt like a heavy blanket wrapped around her. She had been in the city just over a week and spent that entire time in her room, enjoying the air conditioning and looking at her Toronto Maple Leafs collectibles.

The Kimura family had been living in Toronto for Emma's entire life before they packed up everything and moved to Las Vegas. Each of her collectibles reminded her of home, the icy rinks, and the chilly winters. While rebuilding the Lego Friends sets she had to dismantle when they left Canada, she often lost herself in the memories of her old room.

They moved because her mother was offered a golden opportunity to work at a prestigious casino in Las Vegas. Emma didn't have any friends yet, and with the vast desert surrounding her and school yet to start, she was lonely. The mornings felt long and the evenings even longer.

Every day she had been in Las Vegas so far it was as hot as an oven outside, so the cool air conditioning of her house was the only way to stay comfortable.

Unfortunately, Emma was really bored. Rebuilding old Lego sets was an okay distraction from her boredom, but Emma liked being around other kids. The problem with Las Vegas in the summer was that it was really hard to find other kids to play with. Nobody was playing outside in her neighborhood, no kids were at the playgrounds, and there really weren't a lot of other kid things to do in the city. Emma missed Toronto. A lot.

It was a Thursday morning when Emma's dad Ryota came into the room. His face looked concerned but hopeful. "Emma, I know it's been tough for you since we left Toronto, but I've got a surprise for you."

Her interest piqued, Emma perked up. "What is it, Dad?" she asked with a curious tilt in her voice.

With a broad grin, he declared, "I signed you up for hockey. It starts on Saturday." Emma's eyes widened, and a confused look settled on her face as her dad spoke. The idea was so out of left field.

"But Dad, I don't know how to play hockey." Emma was a big fan of the Maple Leafs, being from Toronto and all, but she had never played a minute of hockey in her entire life.

"Well, the program is called 'Girls' Learn to Play' and they even provide equipment you can use to get started. The first practice is on Saturday morning, so we have to go to the rink today to get you all the gear you'll need." Emma was a mix of excited and hesitant. Hockey was her favorite sport to watch, but she was scared about being on the ice as a player.

They drove to the rink, which was an older building attached to a bar. It had two sheets of ice and smelled like rubber and popcorn. The pro shop was right by the entrance and Emma walked in with her dad and immediately became overwhelmed by all the pads, jerseys, and accessories. "Dad, how are we gonna pick out the right equipment?" Emma asked as a teenage boy in a Las Vegas Golden Knights jersey and a hockey mullet approached them.

"You guys here for the LTP program?" he asked Emma.

"LTP? What's that?" Emma was confused.

"Learn to play. You're here to get your equipment, right?"

"Oh yeah, LTP means Learn to play. Duh. Yeah, I need hockey stuff," Emma said as she touched all of the sticks on the rack one by one. "How do I know what I need? There's so much stuff here."

"Don't worry, baby girl, I got you." He started piling up pads on the counter. They all looked so tiny and yet so big at the same time.

Emma stood in stunned silence as the boy stacked the pads up. There was just so much and she didn't think she would know how to put them on. "I'm not sure I'll know how to put all these pads on."

"Don't worry, coach will be there to help you girls out," he said as Ryota paid for the gear and Emma stood next to him as still as a statue.

As Emma and her dad walked out of the pro shop with her brand new hockey bag, Emma was silent.

Emma didn't say anything the whole fifteen-minute ride home and sat in stunned silence on the couch when they got home. Ryota wasn't sure why, but he decided to leave her alone and let her first process it all by herself. Emma was just overwhelmed with how much stuff she would have to put on. Was it really so dangerous to play hockey that she'd need so much more padding than when she rode her bike? Do they allow hitting? Why do we have giant pads on the back of our gloves? Her mind was racing with questions the rest of the week. She could barely wait until the first practice on Saturday morning.

Chapter 2:
The First Practice

Emma barely slept the rest of the week as she waited for Saturday. Getting ready to go to practice in the morning, Emma's mom Jasmine cooked up French toast, scrambled eggs, hash browns, bacon, and kiwi slices—all of Emma's favorite things to eat for breakfast. She barely ate anything on her plate, though. Her stomach was in knots because she was so nervous about playing hockey for the first time. Emma was not a very good ice skater, despite being Canadian, and she had only played street hockey in her shoes, never on skates. It took almost a half an hour for her dad to put on her gear and then her mom made her pose for pictures. A lot of pictures.

"Mom, that's enough pictures. I gotta get on the ice," an exasperated Emma pleaded to her mother. Finally, her mother stopped taking pictures and Emma stepped out onto the ice. And immediately fell on her butt. She got up. And immediately fell right back down again. She crawled over to the wall and grabbed on and pulled herself up. Just then a much taller girl came skating over like she was in fast forward.

"First time on the ice?" She asked, sympathetically.

"Not really, but it's the first time without my parents holding me up," Emma replied as she grabbed back onto the wall, leaning against it.

"Here, straighten your ankles. You won't be able to skate with them bent like that. Hold onto the boards until you don't feel wobbly and then you can skate. It's not as hard as it looks." The girl said this as she bent down to adjust Emma's feet. "I'm Charlotte. I've been playing here for a while, so I can help you out."

"Hi Charlotte, I'm Emma." The rest of the practice, Charlotte and Emma were together, with Charlotte helping her with every little challenge she faced. Having Charlotte was like having an extra coach just for her, and Emma loved it. Emma struggled a lot the whole practice, but each time she fell or made a mistake, Charlotte was there to help. Emma could tell that they would become best friends.

A whistle blew and all the girls rushed to the area in front of the penalty boxes. Emma struggled to find her footing and stumbled over, falling flat on her face as she got close to the huddle. Nobody laughed at her, which was a surprise to

Emma, and she just picked herself up and got on one knee like the other girls.

"Hi, everyone, I'm coach Bella Hooks and I'm in charge of the Las Vegas Queens, our girls program here at the rink. Every one of you will play for the Queens in our house league, and as you get better, you will eventually get to play for the travel team that goes to tournaments out of state." The mention of the travel team got some of the girls really excited and they looked at each other as Coach Bella continued to speak.

"Some of you have played for a while and some of you are just starting, so remember that your teammate may not be in the same part of her hockey journey as you are. Help each other out, be a good teammate to everyone out here, and not just the players you think are good. Work hard and, most of all, have fun. Hockey is the best sport because it's fun, so that's what we are here to do." She said as Emma and her teammates squirmed as they struggled to balance on one knee.

Coach Bella was a hero to a lot of the girls. Her portrait hung on the wall of the rink because she played for the US Women's National Team when she was younger and she scored a goal in the Olympics. Emma thought she was so cool.

The hour of practice went by very quickly with Charlotte helping her with every drill and when coach Bella blew the whistle to signal the final huddle, Emma was drenched in sweat and exhausted, but energized at the same time. Coach Bella said some things, but Emma was too amped up to listen, and when everyone cheered "Go Queens!," Emma just stood there, staring off into space. When she walked off the ice, she was still in a daze. She moved slowly and was very quiet.

"Did you like it?" her dad asked. She nodded.

"Was it fun?" her mom asked. She nodded.

Her parents kept trying to get her to speak up, but Emma sat silently as her dad took her gear off. They went to the car and her dad asked if she wanted ice cream, and she again only nodded.

Emma got an ice cream cone at her new favorite ice cream spot and once it was about halfway finished, she started to talk about her new friend Charlotte.

"And Charlotte told me all about the house league and how we get to play against the boys." Emma went on and on about Charlotte and her brothers and how she and Charlotte were "BFFs" already. Her parents were pleased and gave each other a look as if to say "thank you, hockey."

As soon as they got home, Emma asked to go into the back yard and practice hockey. Ryota and Emma spent an hour passing a street hockey puck back and forth. Emma was hooked. The whole week before the next practice, Emma dragged her dad outside for hockey practice, sometimes for a few hours at a time. Emma wanted to be better by her second practice, but she did not get onto the ice that whole week, so her skating could not improve.

Emma was so determined to improve at hockey before she saw her new friend Charlotte again. She took her stick outside and found a tennis ball in the dog park in their complex and began to do laps in her shoes around their community, stickhandling the tennis ball the whole time. Emma was extremely determined to impress Charlotte at practice on Saturday.

Ryota noticed how much Emma was enjoying her hockey practice, so he went online and ordered a few surprises for her. On Tuesday, they arrived in the mail. In the box was a mini hockey goal, a few outdoor pucks and some targets for shooting practice. He wanted to make sure Emma knew how much he was behind her new interest in hockey and was eager to give her the box.

"Emma! I've got a surprise for you" She was already in front of him before he finished saying "...for you."

"What is it, Dad?" she asked as her eyes focused on the box.

"Open it up and take a look," he said as she wasted no time in tearing open the box and flinging its contents onto the floor. "We can practice in the back yard now. I hope you like it."

"Thanks so much, Daddy!" She immediately took the new equipment outside to set up. For the rest of the week, she was outside practicing every moment she had available to do so. By Friday, she had been outside for at least a dozen hours working on her shot, and she could actually hit a slapshot into the target at a rate of about 1 in 3. She couldn't wait to show Charlotte at practice the next day.

Chapter 3:
Getting Into a Routine

As her family arrived at the rink on Saturday for practice, Emma was giddy with excitement. She had been practicing so hard and wanted to show off the results of her efforts. At practice, she played so well. Coach Bella praised her improvement, especially noting her improved control with the puck. The coach even gave her a few chances to shoot at the goal during a practice scrimmage, and to everyone's amazement, she managed to score a goal.

Charlotte, with a wide grin on her face, skated over. "Looks like someone's been practicing," she teased.

Emma blushed, proud of her achievement. "I wanted to get better, and I had some help," she replied, glancing over at her father who was beaming with pride from the sidelines.

After practice, several parents approached Ryota, inquiring about Emma's sudden improvement. Ryota showed them the mini-hockey goal set he had purchased. Before long, other parents were looking into getting similar sets for their children, hoping it would have the same impact. Over the next few weeks, the routine solidified.

Mornings would start with a hearty breakfast, followed by school. But as soon as school was over, Emma would rush home, change, and head straight to the back yard to practice her hockey. Ryota would often join her, relishing in their bonding time over hockey. The sounds of hockey in the back yard became a comforting backdrop in their household.

One day, Charlotte came over after school, bringing her hockey stick. The two girls spent hours playing and practicing in the back yard. It was evident that their friendship was flourishing, not just on the ice, but off it as well. As the preseason progressed, Emma's skill level dramatically improved. It wasn't just her ability to shoot; she had better control, could manoeuvre better on the ice, and displayed a level of confidence she hadn't shown before. Her bond with Charlotte also played a significant role in this; they pushed each other to be better, and their synergy on the ice was unmatched.

Emma realized that determination, practice, and having the right support system were the ingredients to success. She might have started her hockey journey with a fall, but she was now skating her way to triumph, with a brand new best friend by her side.

Practice became her favorite part of the week and the team was improving with each time on the ice, but the season was starting in a couple of weeks and they would be playing against the boys. The girls were good, but most of the boys had been playing longer and some of them were really skilled. The girls were worried that they would be embarrassed by the boys, so they worked extra hard in the weeks leading up to the game.

Emma started to develop her stickhandling a lot more and loved to pass to Charlotte because Charlotte was a very good finisher. After receiving a pass from Emma, Charlotte would do the rest of the work and get Emma an assist.

Getting assists became Emma's favorite part of hockey. It was still hard for her to score goals, but when a teammate did because of her pass, Emma would feel a jolt of excitement for having contributed to her teammate's success. Passing was something that was easy to do and it would result in great things if done well, so Emma started working on it every single day. She would set up her dog's toys all over the yard and then hit her tennis ball with her stick between two of them, trying to improve her accuracy.

Her dog, a Golden Retriever named Cherry, found this game to be very confusing. She kept getting her toys and then Emma would tell her "no!" and she would be sad that she couldn't play with them. Emma realized that Cherry was not enjoying her game, so she started to involve the dog in her drills. Sometimes Cherry would be on defense, trying to steal the ball, and sometimes she would be a teammate that Emma would pass to. Cherry seemed to really enjoy playing hockey, too, and Emma started calling her "Air Bud" after the Golden Retriever from the movies who played sports.

Her daily games with Cherry made her much more skilled with the stick and Emma became a better player thanks to her canine training partner. It was also really beneficial for Cherry to train with Emma because she became a much better-behaved dog due to her extended playtime on the Sport Court. Cherry learned to be a goalie dog, too, focusing on the puck and catching it in her mouth when Emma was able to shoot it off the ground. Her new goalie made Emma feel more comfortable practicing her shot and she was able to develop a better shot. Emma and Cherry trained together any time Charlotte couldn't be there to practice.

At practice, Emma's teammates Zoey and Ariel noticed her vast improvement in the weeks since they started. Ariel noticed Emma's improving shot the most because she was the goalie. Emma loved playing hockey and loved being a part of the Las Vegas Queens hockey team, but the thing she loved the most was simply being around so many fun and cool girls.

She wasn't lonely in Las Vegas anymore, and one of her new teammates was even from Toronto just like her. For the first time since she came to the United

States from Canada, she felt like she was home.

Chapter 4:
Zoe

The Queens worked extremely hard in the days leading up to their opening game against the Thunder. The Thunder were not a strong team, placing 7th in the league last season, but 7th was still one spot above the Queens who came in dead last. Some of the parents had suggested that the Queens disband and the girls get distributed to the other teams so the girls could win some games, but Charlotte, Sofia, and Zoe (the remaining players on the team from last season) were adamant that they remain an all-girls squad and that they would win games this season.

Zoe was tiny, the smallest girl on the team, but that didn't stop her from being the most aggressive player on the ice any time she was out there. Off the ice, she was a playful girl who loved climbing and hanging upside down, leaving her braids dangling. She loved playing tag with her little brother and was obsessed with Hello Kitty. On the ice, she was like the Tasmanian Devil, causing a path of destruction everywhere she went.

She wasn't the best at controlling the puck, but she excelled at scoring goals because she never gave up on the puck. Zoe was a leader on the bench too, where she constantly cheered on her teammates and kept the bench energy up all game. That is why Zoe had the "A" on her jersey, signifying her as an assistant captain of the Queens.

Zoe started playing hockey as soon as she could get a pair of skates that weren't too big for her. Her dad played hockey a couple of times a week and Zoe would go to his games any time she could. Until she started playing hockey herself, her favorite thing in the world was watching her dad play.

He moved so fast on the ice and with such power. He wasn't the biggest guy, but he was always one of the best on the ice.

He played hard, never gave up on the play, and wasn't afraid to put his body on the line to help set up a goal on offense or save one on defense. Zoe had been watching him play for years and clearly tried to model her own style after his.

When she turned five, she asked her dad to sign her up for hockey lessons, but they couldn't find a set of skates and pads small enough for her to wear. She had to wait another 18 months before they could get her into a set of hockey gear that fit. She signed up for the Girls' Learn to Play program and began her hockey journey. Zoe was a natural on the ice.

She used her lack of height to her advantage and would bend her knees so much when skating that she would shrink to half the size of the other players. This allowed her to push really hard and made her very fast on the ice. Her size also made her hard to defend and made her really good at swooping in and grabbing the puck when it was being fought over. She was a shy girl off the ice, but on the ice she was a voice of authority and was never afraid of any situation.

Zoe was also a joker. She loved trash talking other teams but not in a mean way. She would try to make her opponents laugh and get them off their guard so she could take advantage. She'd say funny words, make funny sounds, and say things about the parents and referees that she thought would make anyone laugh. During practice, she loved to "chirp," which is a hockey term for talking trash, but she'd do it playfully to make her teammates laugh.

Zoe was a fun kid to have around and

everyone on the team considered her a friend. That was another reason for the "A" on her jersey—she was simply a very popular kid on the team. When Emma joined the team, Zoe was second only to Charlotte in welcoming her to the group.

As a player, Zoe was a forward who focused more on getting the puck in her control than she was in putting the puck into the net. She was always eager to chase after the puck into the corners and played with a strength that was huge in comparison to her small size. She was also a skilled passer who would find her teammates open and send the puck right over to them. With her on the ice, the Queens would always have someone willing to make the hard plays.

Away from hockey, Zoe's love for the sport never faded. Her room was a shrine to the game, with posters of her favorite players, and a special corner dedicated to mementos from her own matches—including pucks from significant games and pictures with her teammates. Yet, amidst all the memorabilia, the most treasured item was a photo of a young Zoe, hand-in-hand with her dad, both in their hockey gear, ready to hit the ice.

Her bond with her father was special, transcending their shared love for the sport. He was her mentor, her confidant, and her biggest cheerleader. Their post-game discussions were a ritual, breaking down plays, celebrating successes, and brainstorming on areas of improvement. It was evident that the fire in Zoe's game was ignited by the passion she inherited from her father.

The Queens' roster had seen many players come and go over the years, each bringing their own strengths. But Zoe brought more heart onto the ice than most. She epitomized what it meant to be a Queen—fierce determination, boundless spirit, and an unwavering commitment to the team. Her legacy was just beginning, and the Queens were all the better for having Zoe among their ranks.

Chapter 5: Charlotte

Charlotte had been playing hockey even before she could walk. She was literally holding a hockey stick from the hour she was born. Her dad was a lifelong hockey fan but never played himself and her mom was from a Minnesota family with cousins, aunts, and uncles who all played some level of ice hockey.

Her mom's brother, Uncle Parker had gotten a tiny stick customized at an engraver when she was born with her date of birth, her weight, and her name on it, and he brought it to her in the hospital before she could even hold onto it. The very first picture of Charlotte posted to social media after she was born was of her "holding" the stick in her hands just 75 minutes after she emerged from her mother's belly. Simply put, Charlotte was born to play hockey.

As she learned to walk, she learned to master all the hockey skills, and when she was big enough to fit into a pair of ice skates, she was immediately skating on the ice. Charlotte played with the boys and learned to shoot, stickhandle, skate, and pass better than any of the girls her age. She didn't have any brothers or sisters, so her family saw her as the next great hockey player in the Nguyen family.

Even though Charlotte had talent, she worked very hard. She was always the first one to practice and the last one to leave. Everyone on her team looked up to her. She was a quiet leader. Compared to Zoe's loud mouth and comedic nature, Charlotte was more focused and liked to lead by example and a helping hand. On days when they had games, while others were nervous, Charlotte was always calm and ready to play.

When she wasn't playing hockey, Charlotte was just like any other 8-year-old. She loved ice cream and cartoons. She had lots of toys, but her favorite was a stuffed penguin named Puck. Even though her family cheered for the Minnesota Wild (the top professional team in Minnesota), Charlotte had always loved the Pittsburgh Penguins, because her favorite all-time player was Mario Lemieux. That's why she wore #66—to be just like him. Puck wasn't just any old penguin—he was a Pittsburgh Penguin and Charlotte wrote "66" on his back in Sharpie when her mom gave him to her after she scored her first ever goal in a game.

    Charlotte and her mom were very

close. They both loved hockey a lot. Sometimes, they went to Minnesota to see their family and play hockey on frozen lakes. Charlotte loved hearing stories about her mom and Uncle Parker playing hockey. She felt proud and wanted to be as good as them one day. She was well on her way, being the best 8-year-old girl in her entire city and probably one of the best in the entire nation.

Charlotte took great pride in being a top player and never felt like anything could stop her from success on the ice. She was determined, strong-willed, and a great skater. She could even shoot the puck like one of the older kids, lifting it off the ice and sending it in a line to the back of the net. During her 7-year-old season, Charlotte was the only girl who scored more than one goal in a game and the only one with more than three goals for the whole season, despite being younger than most of the girls on the team.

She didn't have brothers or sisters, but her hockey team, the Las Vegas Queens, were like family. She always stood up for them and made sure they felt important. That is why she befriended Emma when the Learn to Play session started. She saw how hard it was for Emma just to stand up, and instead of letting her fail, Charlotte decided to help her become great. Emma was new in town and didn't have any friends yet, so Charlotte became her very first Las Vegas friend. Emma was fun to spend time with and always said nice things to her, so Charlotte liked her immediately.

Emma looked up to Charlotte, but

she wasn't the only one. People in Las Vegas talked about Charlotte a lot. They saw her as a hope for other young hockey players in the city. For a city that was only recently obsessed with the sport, the early standouts could really create a legend around themselves if they played well enough.

Charlotte's team lost every game and often by large margins, but she was always a bright spot. She scored some really impressive goals that nobody else in her league could, whether it was any of the boys or any of the girls.

Charlotte watched hundreds of hours of YouTube clips of hockey players, especially the talented scorers like Connor Bedard, Alex Ovechkin, Wayne Gretzky, Paul Kariya, and Mario Lemieux. Her favorite video of all, however, was the shootout performance of T.J. Oshie against the Russian team in the 2014 Olympics.

While Lemieux was her favorite all-time player, and Bedard was her favorite current player, the video of Oshie taking on the Russians and single-handedly winning the game for the United States in a legendary shootout was the one she watched over and over again. She imitated every one of his four successful shots, and she developed a similar level of skill on the shootout because of that.

In the 8U level in youth hockey, they closed out the games with a shootout so every kid on both teams would have a chance to try and score in front of the crowd. Charlotte never missed. She scored in all 12 games as a 7-year-old during those shootouts and had already earned a reputation of being the best shootout scorer in the city for her age group.

Charlotte had a bright future in ice hockey, but she wanted to share it with her friends, so Charlotte did everything she could to make her teammates better, especially the new ones who joined the Learn to Skate program. So, when Charlotte saw Emma fall on her first day, she immediately skated over and helped Emma up. She wanted to make Emma feel like a part of the team, not just a new kid who was still learning how to skate.

Charlotte and Emma spent every minute on the ice side by side, with Charlotte working directly with Emma on every little struggle she faced.

Chapter 6: Ariel

Goalies are different. It takes a special kind of person to crouch on the ice and let people shoot hockey pucks at them. Ariel Taylor was that kind of special. Ariel was born to be a goalie. Her dad was a goalie and his dad was one, too. She grew up watching videos of her dad in the minor leagues, making saves and winning games. He never made it to the NHL, though, because he was injured before he got the chance and had to retire from playing. So, Travis Taylor focused his energy on helping his daughter achieve anything she wanted. Thankfully for him, what Ariel wanted was to be the best goalie in Las Vegas.

Every morning before school, Ariel would ask her dad to help her practice in the living room using crumpled up wads of paper. He'd shoot them at her and she would try to stop them. Travis loved this part of the day, and they were often late getting out of the front door in the morning on the way to school.

Ariel's mom, Nicole, was an elite skier when she was younger, but a crash one day ended her career. Her injury was so bad that she could no longer walk. Instead, she used a wheelchair to get around. Nicole loved following Ariel's games, but getting to the rink was really difficult because it wasn't very wheelchair accessible, so most of the time Ariel would get a ride to practices and games from a teammate while her parents would stay at home and watch the games and practices on the rink's live stream.

During these streams, Travis would describe all the action like a play-by-play announcer on a TV broadcast. This way, he hoped Nicole wouldn't feel like she was missing out on anything. She had gone to see Ariel play at the rink a couple of times, but the challenges with accessibility caused Nicole to decide that watching from home would be better. For Ariel, this meant that she was always alone at her games and practices, but knowing her parents were watching from home always made her work extra hard.

Being a goalie is really hard, especially when you don't have help getting all your pads on, but Ariel learned how to get herself fully geared up by age 7. The harder part was simply carrying the gear into the locker room. Thankfully her equipment bag had wheels to roll it through the rink, but it was still big enough that Ariel could hide inside it with room to spare. The other Queens knew about Ariel's challenges, but Ariel never needed their help—she was as independent as a kid her age could be.

Because the rink's video system was always broadcasting during practices and games, Ariel was very aware that she was being watched. She loved to show off, though, so she played extra hard, even during practices. This made her an awesome goalie, or at least someone who was always trying really hard and challenging her teammates.

Being new, Emma struggled to score on Ariel at first, either missing the net entirely or shooting it weakly into Ariel's pads. But, as Emma began to get better, thanks to her training sessions with Cherry and the help she was getting from Charlotte and her other teammates, Emma started to give Ariel a bit more trouble during shootouts. It was Emma's eighth practice when she finally shot a puck past Ariel into the back of the net.

"Great shot, rookie!" Ariel said to

Emma after her first goal. Rookie was the nickname Ariel called Emma by, but she was the only one who called Emma that. Ariel and Emma got along really well and would often chat with each other during water breaks.

As the practice wrapped up, Emma skated over to Ariel, still beaming from her successful shot. "Thanks for cheering me on earlier. You're an amazing goalie. You make it so tough!"

Ariel flashed a grin, pulling off her helmet. "Well, rookie, you're getting pretty good yourself. Keep it up, and I'll have to work even harder to stop your shots!"

The two friends laughed, their breaths visible in the chilly air of the ice rink. Ariel carefully grabbed her water bottle and her backup stick from the bench, looked up at the camera and waved to her parents. Playing well gave her the familiar feeling of pride and joy of being on the ice. She always knew her parents were watching, cheering her on from their cozy living room, making her feel less alone and more motivated to succeed.

As Ariel and Emma exited the rink, the lights of the Las Vegas Strip shined in the distance, reminding Ariel of the countless dreams she harbored. Each day, with every save and every challenge, Ariel was not only following in her family's footsteps, but also skating her own path, writing her own story, one save at a time.

As she got into the car with Victoria Gonzalez, one of the players on defense and her usual carpool partner, she couldn't wait to get back on the ice again, to feel the thrill of the game and the support of her team and family. For now, though, she was content to share the back seat with a friend and teammate. The end of practice wasn't a conclusion—it was a promise of more adventures, more challenges, and more dreams to chase. For Ariel Taylor, every day was a chance to be the special kind of goalie she was born to be.

Chapter 7: Gameday

The Queens had been together for a month when Coach Bella called them into a huddle at the end of practice.

"Girls, you've been working really hard these past four weeks. Now it's time to see what all that hard work has done for you. Next practice we are having a scrimmage with the Kings." The Kings were one of the teams the boys played on at the rink.

"You will wear your game uniforms and socks and be ready to play for real."

The girls all burst into chatter as they excitedly spoke to their nearest teammate.

"Quiet!" Coach Bella yelled, snapping every girl to attention. "We need to work hard and play as a team. Last year they beat us reality badly every time we played them."

"Yeah they did," Charlotte said under her breath to Zoe, two of the only players who played against them the last season.

The Kings were the league runners-up last season and were much better than the Thunder, who were going to be the Queen's first opponent in league play. But playing the Kings was still a good test for the Queens because they would play each other eventually during the season.

"The Kings have some really good players, including Victoria's brother and Grace's brother, so we gotta work really hard to stay in the game," Coach Bella said as she walked them through the game plan. When the Queens were dismissed to the locker room, Emma stayed behind.

"Coach?" Emma said meekly.

"Yes, Emma?" Coach said as she skated closer to Emma.

"I'm scared. I don't want to let my teammates down on Sunday. I've never played a game before."

"There's a first time for everything. The first time that Marie-Philip Poulin hit the ice as a young girl in Canada, do you think she was already the best player in the world? Of course not. She was a beginner just like you, trying to keep up with her older brother as a young girl in Quebec. But by the time she was 18, she was already on the national team of Canada. She wasn't born as 'Captain Clutch.' She became the best player because she worked hard, she didn't give up, and she never let a boy tell her what she couldn't do."

Coach Bella told Emma all of this as she pointed over to a Canadian flag.

"You're a Canadian, so hockey is in

your blood and you've already improved so much since you started here last month. It'll be hard, but you'll be great."

Emma took a deep breath, nodded at her coach and skated off the ice and went to the locker room.

The next two days were a blur as Emma watched every single YouTube video on Marie-Philip Poulin she could find. Her favorite one was when she won the IIHF Women's World Championship in 2021 with a shot off the far post in overtime. Her confidence under pressure was inspiring and Emma felt so proud to be a Canadian just like Marie-Philip.

The night before the game, Emma went to sleep and had nonstop dreams about playing for the Canadian national team and scoring the game-winning goal against Russia, the United States, Sweden, Mexico, Mars, Pandora—even against a team full of hockey-playing kangaroos in Australia. Emma was inspired and ready to play in her very first game.

When her alarm went off in the morning, Emma sprung out of bed as if she was on an ejector seat. She ate a huge breakfast: two Pop Tarts, an Eggo Waffle, scrambled eggs, bacon, and a huge glass of orange juice. Her dad came downstairs wearing a shirt with Queen Elizabeth II on it and Emma couldn't help but laugh.

"Dad, why are you wearing a shirt with the Queen of England on it?"

"Well, what team do you play for?" he asked her.

"The Queens," Emma replied.

"Exactly!" Her dad laughed as he grabbed a piece of bacon and shoved the whole thing into his mouth at once.

Emma got to the rink before any of her teammates, so she sat in the quiet of the locker room, her dad lacing up her skates as she was visualizing the game. She imagined herself skating fast, dodging the Kings' defense, and making perfect passes. She could almost hear the sound of the puck hitting the net, her teammates cheering, and the satisfaction of a well-played game. The calm before the storm was Emma's favorite part of game day—just her, her gear, and her thoughts.

As the rest of the Queens began to arrive, the locker room buzzed with energy and excitement. Charlotte and Zoe, with their experience from the last season, shared tips with the newer players, while Ariel, always the focused goalie, checked and rechecked her equipment. Emma watched and listened, absorbing the camaraderie and excitement. She felt a sense of belonging with these girls that she hadn't felt since leaving Toronto. The Queens were her team; they were her friends.

"Remember, it's not just about winning," Coach Bella said as she walked into the locker room. "It's about playing our best, supporting each other, and learning from the experience."

Her words resonated with Emma, reminding her that this was more than just a game—it was a chance to grow, to challenge herself, and to be part of something bigger. As they headed out to the ice, Emma's heart raced with anticipation. The rink, usually a place of practice and learning, now felt like an arena of challenge and opportunity. She looked up into the stands and saw her dad, still wearing the Queen Elizabeth II shirt, waving a homemade sign that read 'Go Queens!' Her mom was cheering madly next to him. That was the moment Emma knew, no matter what happened on the ice, she was already a winner. She was part of a team, part of a family. She was a Queen.

Chapter 8:
The First Scrimmage

The Queens warmed up and looked across the ice at the Kings. They seemed faster and their shots sounded louder than the Queens. They were one of the best teams last season, so it was going to be a tough game. Emma was especially intimidated by them because she had never played against boys before. She could see DeShaun, her linemate Grace Thompson's twin brother, taking slap shots and skating faster than she'd ever seen another kid skate. Lily Patel, the Queen's backup goalie, was talking to a player on the Kings who Emma recognized as Lily's brother Rohan.

Zoe saw this, too, and skated over and said to Lily, "Don't communicate with the enemy before a game," and then laughed as she skated away.

Coach Bella had the team huddle around a whiteboard with the outline of a hockey rink on it and began to go over the positions and lines for the game. The starting lineup would be Ariel in the goal, the "Sofies"—Sofia Linksy and Sophia Kim—on defense, and Olivia Martinez and Zoe at the wings with Charlotte as the center.

The second line was Victoria Gonzalez and Abigail Patton on D, Elizabeth Callow and Chloe Singh as the forwards, and Grace as the center. The third line was Madison LaFleur and Emily Wong on D, Emily's older sister Ella and Emma as the forwards, and Jocelyn Rodriguez as the center. Lily would be the backup goalie and would probably only play during the second period.

The players lined up on the ice with Charlotte to take the faceoff against DeShaun. The referee dropped the puck and DeShaun got to it first and was able to pass off to Rohan. Rohan skated the puck up on the left side of the ice and his linemates followed close behind him and to his right. He made a fast move and got right past the Sofies. Now that he was one-on-one with Ariel, Rohan took a quick shot and it hit the back of the net. It was already 1-0 and only fourteen seconds had ticked off the clock.

The next faceoff had essentially the same result, but this time it was DeShaun who took the puck in for the goal. 2-0, and still only a minute into the game. The Queens substituted in the second line and the Kings continued to dominate, scoring another goal, making it 3-0.

Emma sat on the bench watching her team get dominated, and she began to lose all of the confidence her dreams from the previous night had given her. She was scared to go out on the ice, and Coach Bella saw the worried look on her face.

"Don't worry, Emma, you'll do great. We're already losing pretty bad, so you can't let us down. Just go out there and try your hardest," Bella said right before she called out, "LINE CHANGE!" and pushed Emma out onto the ice through the open door.

The game felt ten times faster on the ice than it did on the bench, and Emma was immediately overwhelmed. She stood still, staring over at the action about 20 feet away on the ice. As the play continued, Ella hit the puck loose and it slid right past Emma. She didn't even see it as Isaac Jackson pushed her over and took control of it, gliding down the ice towards the goal and hitting a slapshot into the back of the net as Emma lay on the ice watching it all happen. 4-0. After scoring the goal, Isaac skated over to Emma and stood over her.

"That's why girls shouldn't play hockey," he said as he laughed and skated away.

The next minute of Emma's first shift on the ice was uneventful after that. She basically just skated around, but that helped her get over the play where Isaac knocked her over.

When she skated over to the bench, Chloe turned to her and said, "Don't worry, I'll give him a push if I get a chance. Isaac is such a jerk. I go to school with him and he's such a bully."

That made Emma feel better. It meant her teammates supported her no matter what happened, and it gave her the feeling that she could make mistakes and they wouldn't get angry with her over them.

The first period ended with the score at 5-0, and Coach Bella spoke to the Queens during the break between periods.

"Girls, that was a rough start, but we only gave up one goal in the second half of the period. If we can keep up that momentum, that'll be a great place to build from for the season. Remember, this game doesn't count, it is just a scrimmage."

The girls came in for a cheer and then the second period started. On the first shift, Sofia stole the puck from DeShaun and passed it up to Charlotte, who sped up the side of the ice. As Charlotte skated right at the King's defenseman, he stumbled over his own feet and fell over. She was able to get past him and take a shot at the net. GOAL! It was now 5-1.

Emma's next shift was different from her first few during the first period. She was more comfortable with the speed of the game and kept her head up more. She hit the puck a few times but didn't get control at any point. It felt good to her, though; she didn't feel out of place anymore.

The second period was much more even than the first as the boys got a bit tired and the girls gained confidence. The Queens were fighting for the puck more and keeping the Kings from getting any real scoring opportunities. Emma played three shifts that period, and each shift she was more confident than the last. By the third period, Emma felt like a real hockey player.

In the final period, Lily was playing goalie and Charlotte swapped lines with Jocelyn so she could play with Emma. Lily made some good saves, but gave up three goals, so the score was 8-1 with just 2 minutes left. Coach Bella called for a line change and Emma's line went out onto the ice for the last shift of the game.

Having Charlotte skating with her during the third period made Emma feel much more confident and on this shift she was determined to make a good play. Emma's chance came with 38 seconds left on the clock. Johnny Nemour had the puck for the Kings and Emma charged at him, hitting his stick and setting the puck loose. Emma skated at it with all her might and pushed the puck forward with her stick. She was alone on the right side and saw Charlotte on the opposite side of the ice. She passed the puck over to Charlotte, and in one smooth move she received the pass and shot it directly into the top left of the net. GOAL! The score was now 8-2, but Emma felt like it was a game winner because she had gotten the assist.

The game ended soon after that, and even though they lost 8-2, the Queens went into the locker room feeling good about themselves. Coach Bella brought them all together for a post-game talk.

"Girls, you guys worked really hard those last two periods. You didn't give up and you showed those boys that you're not going to back down. They only outscored us three to two in those last two periods.

Great job, Charlotte, scoring both of our goals, and awesome work, Emma, on getting that assist near the end of the game."

They came together for a cheer and then got back into their street clothes and left the locker room. Emma was energized and hyper about the game as she left the rink with her parents.

"Can we get ice cream? Please?" she pleaded.

"After the way you played today, you can have a whole sundae! I am so proud of you Emma," Jasmine said as she helped Emma put her gear into the car.

Ryota started the car and they drove to the ice cream place just a block away from the rink. As usual for a Saturday afternoon in the summer, there was a huge line, and many of the people in line were from the hockey rink. As the Kimura family got into the line, another family got into the line right behind them. It was the Jacksons and Isaac was right in front.

"Of all the people to get into this line, it's him! Bleach!" Emma thought to herself as she saw the bully from the game get behind her in line.

She tried not to make eye contact with him, but he noticed her before she could turn away. He didn't say anything to her while they waited to get their ice cream. Emma got an Ube Honeycomb ice cream, her favorite flavor, and stood by the register waiting for her dad to pay.

"I told you girls shouldn't play hockey. You lost 8-2," Isaac said meanly to her as they walked out the door.

Emma didn't have a comeback and the smile melted off her face as he said that.

As they got into the car, Ryota turned to Emma in the back and said "Some people are mean, but never let their words change the way you feel. Remember how you felt as you left the rink, because that's how you deserve to feel today. I'm so proud of you and can't wait to see how much your team improves the next time you play the Kings."

"Thanks Dad, I can't wait to play those guys again. I'm gonna prove that

Isaac jerk wrong. Girls SHOULD play hockey!"

Appendix: List of Characters

LAS VEGAS QUEENS DEPTH CHART
COACH:
Bella Hooks: Coach and a former National Team player

GOALIES:
STARTER
Ariel Taylor: A white American girl with blonde hair, blue eyes, and a hardworking and determined personality.
BACKUP
Lily Patel: An Indian-American girl with curly black hair, hazel eyes, and a friendly and energetic personality.

DEFENSE:
LINE 1
Sophia Kim: A Korean-American girl with black hair and dark brown eyes, who has a competitive and determined personality on the ice. One of the "Sofies."

Sofia Linsky: A white American girl with blonde hair, brown eyes, and a strong and physical presence on the ice. One of the "Sofies."

LINE 2
Victoria Gonzalez: A Mexican-American girl with brown hair, brown eyes, and a powerful and accurate slapshot.

Abigail Patton: A white American girl with long brown hair, brown eyes, and a persistent and determined attitude on the ice.

LINE 3
Madison LeFleur: A French-Canadian girl with straight black hair, brown eyes, and a calm and composed demeanor on the ice.

Emily Wong (Ella's younger sister): A Chinese-Canadian girl with straight black hair, brown eyes, and a calm and focused demeanor on the ice.

WINGS:
LINE 1
Olivia Martinez: A Mexican-American girl with brown hair, brown eyes, and a quick and creative playmaking ability.
Zoe Williams: ASSISTANT CAPTAIN An African-American girl with braided black hair, brown eyes, and a confident and assertive style of play.
LINE 2
Elizabeth Callow: A white American girl with straight blonde hair, green eyes, and a precise and accurate shot.
Chloe Singh: An Indian-Canadian girl with curly brown hair, brown eyes, and a tenacious and aggressive style of play.
LINE 3
Emma Kimura: A Japanese-Canadian girl with straight black hair, brown eyes, and a quick and agile skating ability.
Ella Wong (Emily's older sister): A Chinese-American girl with straight black hair, brown eyes, and a strong and physical presence on the ice.

CENTERS:
LINE 1:
Charlotte Nguyen: CAPTAIN A Vietnamese-American girl with black hair, brown eyes, and a natural leadership ability on the ice.

LINE 2:
Grace Thompson: A biracial (white and Black) girl with brown hair and green eyes, who is a smart and versatile player on the ice.

LINE 3:
Jocelyn Rodriguez: A Puerto Rican-American girl with curly brown hair, brown eyes, and a creative and unpredictable style of play.

OTHER CHARACTERS:
Jasmine Kimura: Emma's Mom
Ryota Kimura: Emma's dad
Nicole Taylor: Ariel's mom
Travis Taylor: Ariel's dad

Isaac Jackson: Bully who plays forward but is more interested in pushing others around—plays for the Kings.
Johnny Nemour: Defenseman who is in his first season—plays for the Kings.
Rohan Patel: Lily's brother, defensive forward with an eye for the spectacular pass—plays for the Kings.
DeShaun Thompson: Grace's brother, an aggressive and very skilled player who shows no mercy on the ice—plays for the Kings.

Made in the USA
Las Vegas, NV
05 February 2024

85366738R00069